# GRATITUDE JOURNAL FOR
# TEEN GIRLS & MOMS

## SHARED PROMPTS FOR CONNECTION AND JOY

### WHITNEY FLEMING

ROCKRIDGE
PRESS

For general information on our other products and services or to obtain technical support, please contact our Customer Care Department within the United States at (866) 744-2665, or outside the United States at (510) 253-0500.

Rockridge Press publishes its books in a variety of electronic and print formats. Some content that appears in print may not be available in electronic books, and vice versa.

Interior and Cover Designer: Angela Navarra
Art Producer: Samantha Ulban
Editor: Mary Colgan
Production Editor: Andrew Yackira
Production Manager: Michael Kay

Cover Illustration © 2021 Jessica Swift

ISBN: Print 978-1-63807-133-4
R0

For Mark, who never stops encouraging me in every way. It's my privilege to walk beside you in this life. For Payton, Olivia, and Cam, who challenge me to be my best self every single day. And for my sweet mom, who loved me first.

"Gratitude helps you
fall in love with the life
you already have."

—Unknown

# INTRODUCTION

As the mother of three teenage girls, sometimes I get overwhelmed by the busy schedules and evolving personalities under our roof. A friend suggested I start a gratitude journal, and it wasn't until I used it regularly that I noticed how often I was missing out on the beautiful things happening right in front of me! The simple act of writing down the small stuff that brings me joy shifted my mindset and helped me be a more patient, less anxious mother. The teen years can be a challenging time for a mom and daughter to maintain a strong bond, but this journal can help you learn how to incorporate gratitude into your daily life and forge a more peaceful relationship.

## WHY GRATITUDE?

My mom always said there was nothing more powerful than a grateful heart, and she helped me appreciate both what our family had and what others did for us. She subtly incorporated gratitude into every facet of our life, from handwriting thank-you notes after birthday parties, to reminding us to be thankful for the food on our table each night. Science backs my mom up. Neuroscientist Alex Korb, PhD, believes that expressing gratitude activates the same hormone in the brain as when experiencing pleasure. In his book, *The Upward Spiral: Using Neuroscience to Reverse the Course of Depression, One Small Change at a Time*, Korb writes, "One powerful effect of gratitude is that it can boost serotonin," which is also known as the "pleasure hormone."

Practicing gratitude is particularly beneficial for teenagers who face a roller coaster of complex emotions every day. Gratitude can soften the edges of those highs and lows and bring some peace to their evolving world. Grateful kids are happier, more hopeful, and do better in school. More important, they experience less envy, anxiety, and depression. Even doing a few simple journal exercises can help a teen feel calmer and more connected to the people, places, and things around them.

# YOUR JOURNEY BEGINS

It's no secret that gratefulness is good for you, but how do you point your attitude toward gratitude? Gratitude can be challenging, but a shared gratitude journal can help you gain a fresh perspective on what you appreciate. Plus, it will help you and your daughter get to know each other better in a fun, meaningful way.

This journal includes a variety of prompts for both moms and daughters, so you both can become more mindful about the positive things in your life. Some prompts will be lighthearted and silly, and others will allow you to think deeply about important issues, such as self-esteem and relationships.

Before you get started, it's helpful to discuss some basic guidelines. I've provided a few below, but remember: There is more than one way to practice gratitude, and the way you share this book is up to you. The end goal is to help you bring gratitude into your daily life.

**Finding Time.** Your schedules are probably hectic, and adding anything else into the mix may be a challenge. It'll help to commit to a realistic schedule for using the journal, whether it's once a week, twice a week, or twice a month. The important thing is to make it work for you both!

**Be Honest.** This journal should be a safe space for you to share your feelings without judgment. This can be hard for moms and daughters, so make a pact that the journal is a place for open communication.

**Long-Distance Plan.** If you don't live under the same roof, you can still share your gratitude with a little planning. Can you hand off the book each week, or video chat every month? Do you want to mix it up and sometimes email or text your responses? Your relationship is unique, so find what's right for you.

**Keep It Fun!** Gratitude shouldn't be a chore. Be spontaneous and creative with your answers. Savor the surprises you learn about each other. Use the free space to draw funny pictures or write messages of encouragement. Don't worry about spelling or grammar.

**Be Specific.** To keep it fresh, try to use all your senses (for example, think of the smell of popcorn while watching your favorite movie). You could also think about the people involved in something you appreciate, like the person who grinds your coffee beans. Over time, you'll find that details will come easier. There are no limits when it comes to gratitude.

**Take a Break.** Sometimes life gets busy, and this journal could become merely another item on your to-do list. If needed, take a break, and return to this journal when you can focus on it. There is no blue ribbon for being the most grateful, so just do the best you can.

**You Do YOU.** Remember, this is YOUR journal, and you get to make the rules. The positive effects of gratitude are endless, so by making your first entry in this journal, you are starting down the path to a happier, more positive you!

# ON THE SAME PAGE

Are you ready to get started? To make sure you are both on the same page with this journal, answer the following questions honestly. Keep in mind your current commitments and obligations as you answer. This will set the tone for how you work together to incorporate gratitude into your daily lives.

## We started this journal together on

_____

1. What do we hope to get out of this journal?

_____

_____

_____

2. How often do we want to write in it? Let's set a schedule.

_____

_____

_____

3. How much time should we spend on each entry?

_____

_____

_____

4. Should we go through the book in order or skip around?

_____

_____

_____

**5.** Should we discuss the entries? How often?

_____

_____

_____

**6.** What if we want or need to take a break? How will we communicate this?

_____

_____

_____

_____

**7.** Can we be open and honest with each other without judgment?

_____

_____

_____

_____

8.  What if we don't know how to answer a prompt? How
    should we handle this?

    _____

    _____

    _____

    _____


9.  What do we want to learn about each other by doing
    this journal?

    _____

    _____

    _____

    _____

# A NEW LENS

Gratitude is like any new activity you try. The more you practice, the easier it gets.

Gratitude involves noticing and appreciating the good things in your life. Although it sounds simple, it can be difficult to stop dwelling on the bad experiences you have each day. You can do it by training your brain to move its focus off the negative and onto the positive. It won't happen overnight, but by regularly taking just a few minutes to focus on things that bring you joy, you will see a shift in your mindset as you develop an attitude of gratitude!

# MOM

Reflecting on your day is a great way to start incorporating gratitude into your routine. Think about yesterday from start to finish. What was your favorite part of the day?

_____

_____

_____

Name something beautiful that you saw. What did you appreciate about it?

_____

_____

_____

_____

_____

Who made your day better?

_____

_____

_____

Reflecting on your day is a great way to start incorporating gratitude into your routine. Think about yesterday from start to finish. What was your favorite part of the day?

_____

_____

_____

Name something beautiful that you saw. What did you appreciate about it?

_____

_____

_____

_____

_____

Who made your day better?

_____

_____

_____

Describe a memory from when you were a teenager that makes you smile. What are you grateful for about the experience?

_____

_____

_____

_____

_____

_____

_____

_____

_____

_____

_____

_____

Describe a memory that makes you smile. What are you grateful for about the experience?

_____

_____

_____

_____

_____

_____

_____

_____

_____

_____

_____

_____

_____

_____

Write down three new things you learned how to do this year.

_____

_____

_____

## Daughter's response

Why are you proud that your mom learned these things?

_____

_____

_____

_____

_____

_____

_____

_____

# DAUGHTER

Write down three new things you learned how to do this year.

_____

_____

_____

## Mom's response

Why are you proud that your daughter learned these things?

_____

_____

_____

_____

_____

_____

_____

_____

Gratitude for what makes you happy can help you move your focus from the negative to the positive.

What is something that always makes you laugh out loud?

_____

_____

What is something that makes you feel safe and cozy?

_____

_____

_____

_____

No matter what mood you're in, what song always makes you want to dance?

_____

_____

**(Bonus: Play this song in the car on the way to school or at breakfast!)**

# DAUGHTER

Gratitude for what makes you happy can help you move your focus from the negative to the positive.

What is something that always makes you laugh out loud?

_____

_____

What is something that makes you feel safe and cozy?

_____

_____

_____

_____

No matter what mood you're in, what song always makes you want to dance?

_____

_____

**(Bonus: Play this song after dinner or when you're doing a chore!)**

9

# MOM

What is your biggest accomplishment in life so far, and why?
Who helped you along the way?

_____

_____

_____

_____

_____

_____

_____

_____

_____

_____

_____

_____

# DAUGHTER

What is your biggest accomplishment in life so far, and why?
Who helped you along the way?

_____

_____

_____

_____

_____

_____

_____

_____

_____

_____

_____

_____

It's easy to forget to appreciate the small things right in front of us that bring us joy. What is something in your bedroom that makes you happy?

_____

_____

_____

What is your favorite article of clothing?

_____

_____

What is something you love about coming home?

_____

_____

_____

_____

_____

# DAUGHTER

It's easy to forget to appreciate the small things right in front of us that bring us joy. What is something in your bedroom that makes you happy?

_____

_____

_____

What is your favorite article of clothing?

_____

_____

What is something you love about coming home?

_____

_____

_____

_____

_____

_____

# MOM

Free writing space

_____

_____

_____

_____

_____

_____

_____

_____

_____

_____

_____

_____

_____

_____

# DAUGHTER

Free writing space

_____

_____

_____

_____

_____

_____

_____

_____

_____

_____

_____

_____

_____

_____

Where do you feel most relaxed and at peace?

_____

_____

_____

_____

What was your favorite family trip when you were growing up and why?

_____

_____

_____

_____

What is your favorite way to spend time with me?

_____

_____

_____

_____

# DAUGHTER

Where do you feel the most relaxed and at peace?

_____

_____

_____

_____

What is your favorite family trip that we've taken and why?

_____

_____

_____

_____

What is your favorite way to spend time with me?

_____

_____

_____

_____

Describe your perfect day. What would you do, and who would join you?

_____

_____

_____

_____

_____

_____

_____

_____

_____

_____

_____

Describe your perfect day. What would you do, and who would join you?

_____

_____

_____

_____

_____

_____

_____

_____

_____

_____

_____

_____

_____

List four things you couldn't live without.

_____

_____

_____

_____

Choose one of those things and write down all the things you love about it.

_____

_____

_____

_____

_____

_____

_____

_____

List four things you couldn't live without.

_____

_____

_____

_____

Choose one of those things and write down all the things you love about it.

_____

_____

_____

_____

_____

_____

_____

_____

# MOM

What is the best surprise you've ever had? How did it make you feel?

_____

_____

_____

_____

_____

_____

_____

_____

_____

_____

_____

What is the best surprise you've ever had? How did it make you feel?

_____

_____

_____

_____

_____

_____

_____

_____

_____

_____

_____

_____

_____

_____

# MOM

What is your favorite fancy beverage? What do you like about it?

_____

_____

_____

_____

What dessert could you eat every night and never get sick of?

_____

_____

When I want to celebrate, I like to go _____.

It makes me happy because:

_____

_____

_____

_____

_____

# DAUGHTER

What is your favorite fancy beverage? What do you like about it?

_____

_____

_____

_____

What dessert could you eat every night and never get sick of?

_____

_____

When I want to celebrate, I like to go _____.

It makes me happy because:

_____

_____

_____

_____

# MOM

Describe a close friend. What qualities do you appreciate
about them? How do they encourage you?

_____

_____

_____

_____

_____

_____

_____

_____

_____

_____

_____

_____

_____

_____

_____

# DAUGHTER

Describe a close friend. What qualities do you appreciate about them? How do they encourage you?

_____

_____

_____

_____

_____

_____

_____

_____

_____

_____

_____

_____

_____

_____

# MOM

List five qualities about yourself that make you proud.

_____

_____

_____

_____

_____

## Daughter's response

List five qualities about your mom that you appreciate.

_____

_____

_____

_____

_____

# DAUGHTER

List five qualities about yourself that make you proud.

_____

_____

_____

_____

_____

## Mom's response

List five qualities about your daughter that you appreciate.

_____

_____

_____

_____

_____

# MOM

It's easy to forget to celebrate the small wins. I was proud of myself for finishing _____ this week.

What is something kind you did for someone else recently?

_____

_____

_____

_____

_____

What is something you are looking forward to in the next week?

_____

_____

_____

_____

_____

# DAUGHTER

It's easy to forget to celebrate the small wins. I was proud of myself for finishing _____ this week.

What is something kind you did for someone else recently?

_____

_____

_____

_____

_____

What is something you are looking forward to in the next week?

_____

_____

_____

_____

_____

_____

# MOM

Describe a favorite photo of yourself. Why do you love it?
What positive qualities about yourself stand out?

_____

_____

_____

_____

_____

_____

_____

_____

_____

_____

_____

_____

_____

Describe a favorite photo of yourself. Why do you love it?
What positive qualities about yourself stand out?

_____

_____

_____

_____

_____

_____

_____

_____

_____

_____

_____

_____

_____

_____

Free writing space

_____

_____

_____

_____

_____

_____

_____

_____

_____

_____

_____

_____

_____

# DAUGHTER

Free writing space

_____

_____

_____

_____

_____

_____

_____

_____

_____

_____

_____

_____

_____

_____

_____

_____

# THE STORIES YOU TELL

There is a lot of noise coming at you from the out-side world, particularly from the media. It's easy to fall into a comparison trap and forget to see the positives in your life, or to become anxious and over-whelmed about things you cannot control. When external factors impact your internal mood, you can reshape your emotions by focusing on things that you enjoy and that make you happy. When the world gets too loud, it helps to slow down and focus on what is important in the here and now. Practicing gratitude regularly can help.

Something that causes me stress is _____.

This is what helps me relax when I feel stressed.

_____

_____

_____

_____

_____

I enjoy spending time with _____ when I'm
going through a tough time, because I know they understand
me. I appreciate them because:

_____

_____

_____

_____

_____

_____

# DAUGHTER

Something that causes me stress is _____.

This is what helps me relax when I feel stressed.

_____

_____

_____

_____

_____

I enjoy spending time with _____ when I'm going through a tough time, because I know they understand me. I appreciate them because:

_____

_____

_____

_____

_____

_____

# MOM

Describe a typical day in your life. How do you feel about your schedule? What part of your day are you the most thankful for?

_____

_____

_____

_____

_____

_____

_____

_____

_____

_____

_____

_____

# DAUGHTER

Describe a typical day in your life. How do you feel about your schedule? What part of your day are you the most thankful for?

_____

_____

_____

_____

_____

_____

_____

_____

_____

_____

_____

_____

_____

# MOM

List five things that went right this week.

_____

_____

_____

_____

_____

List one thing that went wrong. Can you think of anything good that came out of it?

_____

_____

_____

_____

_____

_____

_____

# DAUGHTER

List five things that went right this week.

_____

_____

_____

_____

_____

List one thing that went wrong. Can you think of anything good that came out of it?

_____

_____

_____

_____

_____

_____

_____

_____

What is something you were recently worried about that turned out okay?

_____

_____

_____

_____

Reflect on that situation. What are you thankful for now that it's over?

_____

_____

_____

_____

What is a chore around the house that you like doing? What do you like about it?

_____

_____

_____

What is something you were recently worried about that turned out okay?

_____

_____

_____

_____

Reflect on that situation. What are you thankful for now that it's over?

_____

_____

_____

_____

What is a chore around the house that you like doing? What do you like about it?

_____

_____

_____

What is something you were afraid to try but are glad you did anyway? What did you learn from it?

_____

_____

_____

_____

_____

_____

_____

_____

_____

_____

_____

_____

_____

# DAUGHTER

What is something you were afraid to try but are glad you did anyway? What did you learn from it?

_____

_____

_____

_____

_____

_____

_____

_____

_____

_____

_____

_____

_____

When you are feeling self-conscious, what is something that makes you feel more confident?

_____

_____

_____

_____

What is something you felt self-conscious about as a kid that you feel better about now?

_____

_____

_____

_____

How can gratitude help you be more confident?

_____

_____

_____

# DAUGHTER

When you are feeling self-conscious, what is something that makes you feel more confident?

_____

_____

_____

_____

What is something you felt self-conscious about when you were younger that you're starting to feel better about?

_____

_____

_____

_____

How can gratitude help you be more confident?

_____

_____

_____

# MOM

Free writing space

_____

_____

_____

_____

_____

_____

_____

_____

_____

_____

_____

_____

_____

_____

Free writing space

_____

_____

_____

_____

_____

_____

_____

_____

_____

_____

_____

_____

_____

# MOM

What is something your friends think you are good at doing?

_____

_____

_____

What is one talent that you're grateful for?

_____

_____

What book or movie has inspired you? What did you appreciate about it?

_____

_____

_____

_____

_____

_____

# DAUGHTER

What is something your friends think you are good at doing?

_____

_____

_____

What is one talent that you're grateful for?

_____

_____

What book or movie has inspired you? What did you appreciate about it?

_____

_____

_____

_____

_____

_____

# MOM

What was your most embarrassing moment as a teen? How did the experience make you stronger?

_____

_____

_____

_____

_____

_____

_____

_____

_____

_____

_____

_____

What was your most embarrassing moment? How did the experience make you stronger?

_____

_____

_____

_____

_____

_____

_____

_____

_____

_____

_____

_____

_____

List five things you loved about being a teenager.

_____

_____

_____

_____

_____

## Daughter's response

Do you love any of the same things your mom did?

_____

_____

_____

_____

_____

_____

# DAUGHTER

List five things you love about being a teenager.

_____

_____

_____

_____

_____

## Mom's response

Did you love any of the same things your daughter does?

_____

_____

_____

_____

_____

_____

# MOM

What is something that happened in the past that you were unhappy about, but now you think it worked out for the best? Why are you grateful it worked out this way?

_____

_____

_____

_____

_____

_____

_____

_____

_____

_____

_____

_____

# DAUGHTER

What is something that happened in the past that you were unhappy about, but now you think it worked out for the best? Why are you grateful it worked out this way?

_____

_____

_____

_____

_____

_____

_____

_____

_____

_____

_____

_____

# MOM

Besides your parents, who was someone that had a positive influence on you when you were a teen?

_____

_____

Is there anyone you had a difficult relationship with as a kid, who you now appreciate?

_____

_____

_____

_____

Who is the most confident person you know in real life? What traits do you share?

_____

_____

_____

_____

# DAUGHTER

Besides your parents, who is someone that has had a positive influence on you?

_____

_____

Is there anyone you have a difficult relationship with, who you also appreciate?

_____

_____

_____

Who is the most confident person you know in real life? What traits do you share?

_____

_____

_____

# MOM

What are you most grateful for, right at this moment? It can be something big, like your family, or small, like your favorite ice cream.

_____

_____

_____

_____

_____

_____

_____

_____

_____

_____

_____

_____

_____

# DAUGHTER

What are you most grateful for, right at this moment? It can be something big, like your family, or small, like your favorite ice cream.

_____

_____

_____

_____

_____

_____

_____

_____

_____

_____

_____

_____

List five simple ways you are fortunate.

_____

_____

_____

_____

_____

## Daughter's response

Is there anything on your mom's list that surprises you? Why or why not?

_____

_____

_____

_____

_____

_____

List five simple ways you are fortunate.

_____

_____

_____

_____

_____

## Mom's response

Is there anything on your daughter's list that surprises you? Why or why not?

_____

_____

_____

_____

_____

# MOM

What amazes you about your daughter?

_____

_____

_____

What is the main way you're alike?

_____

_____

_____

_____

_____

What is one way you wish you were more like your daughter?

_____

_____

_____

_____

# DAUGHTER

What amazes you about your mom?

_____

_____

_____

What is the main way you're alike?

_____

_____

_____

_____

What is one way you wish you were more like your mom?

_____

_____

_____

Describe a time when you felt like you didn't fit in. What did you learn? Did anything good come out of not fitting in?

_____

_____

_____

_____

_____

_____

_____

_____

_____

_____

_____

Describe a time when you felt like you didn't fit in. What did you learn? Did anything good come out of not fitting in?

_____

_____

_____

_____

_____

_____

_____

_____

_____

_____

_____

_____

_____

# MOM

Free writing space

_____

_____

_____

_____

_____

_____

_____

_____

_____

_____

_____

_____

_____

_____

# DAUGHTER

Free writing space

# OUR RESILIENCE

Sometimes in life you can feel overwhelmed by a situation and want to give up. Resilience is the ability to recover from something difficult or unpleasant. It's how you move forward after a challenging event, such as failing a test, not making a team, or even losing a loved one. Gratitude can help you see the positive things during a tough time—and grow as a result. By flipping the narrative, you can rebound faster, build better habits, and feel happier and more satisfied with your life.

When you were a teenager, what was a challenging class in school that you found yourself enjoying? What did you like about it?

_____

_____

_____

_____

Think about someone in your life who had to overcome adversity. What qualities helped them succeed?

_____

_____

_____

_____

When you were a teenager, who could you lean on during a difficult time? Why did you turn to them?

_____

_____

What class has been the most challenging for you? What have you learned from it?

_____

_____

_____

_____

Think about someone in your life who had to overcome adversity. What qualities helped them succeed?

_____

_____

_____

Who can you lean on during a difficult time? Why do you feel you can turn to them?

_____

_____

_____

_____

# MOM

Think about a time in your life when you felt rejected. Was there a silver lining? What did you learn from the experience?

_____

_____

_____

_____

_____

_____

_____

_____

_____

_____

_____

_____

_____

# DAUGHTER

Think about a time in your life when you felt rejected. Was there a silver lining? What did you learn from the experience?

_____

_____

_____

_____

_____

_____

_____

_____

_____

_____

_____

_____

_____

_____

_____

List three things that were hard for you as a teenager that you were able to improve upon with practice.

_____

_____

_____

_____

_____

## Daughter's response

How have you seen your mom's hard work pay off?

_____

_____

_____

_____

_____

_____

List three things that were hard for you in the past but are easier now.

_____

_____

_____

_____

_____

## Mom's response

How have you seen your daughter's hard work pay off?

_____

_____

_____

_____

_____

# MOM

What is something you are good at that your daughter might not know about?

_____

_____

_____

_____

What is something you are good at that you might take for granted?

_____

_____

_____

_____

What's something you're not good at, but you enjoy doing it anyway?

_____

_____

_____

# DAUGHTER

What is something you are good at that your mom might not know about?

_____

_____

_____

_____

What is something you're good at that you might take for granted?

_____

_____

_____

_____

What's something you're not good at, but you enjoy doing it anyway?

_____

_____

_____

What was the hardest thing you experienced in your child-hood? What did you learn from it that made your life better?

_____

_____

_____

_____

_____

_____

_____

_____

_____

_____

_____

_____

What did you think about your mom's response? Has something similar happened to you?

_____

_____

_____

_____

_____

_____

_____

_____

_____

_____

_____

_____

_____

_____

What is something you appreciate about friendship with other women?

_____

_____

_____

_____

Has there been a time when you had a problem with a friend? What did you learn from it?

_____

_____

_____

_____

Has conflict with a friend ever made the relationship stronger? How?

_____

_____

_____

# DAUGHTER

What is something you appreciate about friendship with other girls?

_____

_____

_____

_____

Has there been a time when you had a problem with a friend? What did you learn from it?

_____

_____

_____

_____

Has conflict with a friend ever made the relationship stronger? How?

_____

_____

_____

Free writing space

_____

_____

_____

_____

_____

_____

_____

_____

_____

_____

_____

_____

_____

_____

# DAUGHTER

Free writing space

_____

_____

_____

_____

_____

_____

_____

_____

_____

_____

_____

_____

_____

_____

# MOM

What are some things your body can do that you're grateful for?

_____

_____

_____

_____

How does your body feel in this moment? What do you appreciate about being in your own skin?

_____

_____

_____

_____

How can you show yourself kindness when you're feeling down?

_____

_____

_____

# DAUGHTER

What are some things your body can do that you're grateful for?

_____

_____

_____

_____

How does your body feel in this moment? What do you appreciate about being in your own skin?

_____

_____

_____

_____

How can you show yourself kindness when you're feeling down?

_____

_____

_____

# MOM

Write about a time that you felt jealous of someone else. How can you appreciate yourself more when you feel that way?

_____

_____

_____

_____

_____

_____

_____

_____

_____

_____

_____

_____

# DAUGHTER

Write about a time that you felt jealous of someone else. How can you appreciate yourself more when you feel that way?

_____

_____

_____

_____

_____

_____

_____

_____

_____

_____

_____

_____

# MOM

What are five things that cheer you up when you're feeling sad?

_____

_____

_____

_____

_____

Choose one of those things and write all the things you love about it.

_____

_____

_____

_____

_____

_____

_____

# DAUGHTER

What are five things that cheer you up when you're feeling sad?

_____

_____

_____

_____

_____

Choose one of those things and write all the things you love about it.

_____

_____

_____

_____

_____

_____

_____

# MOM

If you had to leave your home quickly, what one item would you take with you? Why?

_____

_____

_____

_____

_____

_____

_____

_____

_____

_____

_____

_____

If you had to leave your home quickly, what one item would you take with you? Why?

_____

_____

_____

_____

_____

_____

_____

_____

_____

_____

_____

_____

# MOM

What is something that comes easy to you?

_____

_____

What is something you had to work hard at to do well?

_____

_____

What is a positive thing about being naturally good at something?

_____

_____

_____

What is a positive thing about having to work hard to do something well?

_____

_____

_____

What is something that comes easy to you?

_____

_____

What is something you had to work hard at to do well?

_____

_____

What is a positive thing about being naturally good at something?

_____

_____

_____

What is a positive thing about having to work hard to do something well?

_____

_____

_____

# MOM

If you could go back and talk your teenage self through a hard time, what would you tell her?

_____

_____

_____

_____

_____

_____

_____

_____

_____

_____

_____

What do you think about your mom's response? Do you think it's relevant to you today?

_____

_____

_____

_____

_____

_____

_____

_____

_____

_____

_____

What are the top five things on your bucket list?

_____

_____

_____

_____

_____

## Daughter's response

What is one thing on your mom's bucket list that you think would be fun to do with her? Why?

_____

_____

_____

_____

_____

What are the top five things you are looking forward to doing when you live on your own?

_____

_____

_____

_____

_____

## Mom's response

What is one thing on your daughter's list that you think would be fun to do with her? Why?

_____

_____

_____

_____

What is a rule your parents had when you were growing up that you are grateful for now?

_____

_____

_____

What is something you completed this year that you are glad is behind you?

_____

_____

_____

_____

The news can often be filled with negativity. What is something you recently saw online that made you smile?

_____

_____

_____

_____

# DAUGHTER

Are there any rules you have at home that you are grateful for?

_____

_____

_____

Is there something about the last year that you are glad is over?

_____

_____

_____

_____

Sometimes the world can be harsh. What is something you recently saw online that made you smile?

_____

_____

_____

_____

What is the hardest decision you've made so far? Are you happy with the way things turned out?

_____

_____

_____

_____

_____

## Daughter's response

How do you feel about what your mom wrote? Does it surprise you?

_____

_____

_____

_____

_____

What is the hardest decision you've made so far? Are you happy with the way things turned out?

_____

_____

_____

_____

_____

## Mom's response

How do you feel about what your daughter wrote? Does it surprise you?

_____

_____

_____

_____

_____

# MOM

Free writing space

_____

_____

_____

_____

_____

_____

_____

_____

_____

_____

_____

_____

_____

# DAUGHTER

Free writing space

_____

_____

_____

_____

_____

_____

_____

_____

_____

_____

_____

_____

_____

_____

SECTION FOUR

# THE BIGGER PICTURE

There is no limit to what you can be grateful for if you take a moment to pause, observe, and reflect. Once you start noticing the positive aspects of your life, you can begin expanding the breadth of your gratitude to the world around you, especially the small things that many people take for granted. One of the greatest lessons about gratitude I learned was from my own mother. Whenever someone mentioned that she had endured a hard life, she responded, "Oh, no. I've been blessed. I've had it harder than some, but better than most. I've had food to eat, a roof over my head, shoes on my feet, and a family to love. You can't ask for more than that."

# MOM

What is something you want to protect in the environment?

_____

_____

_____

What is your favorite way to enjoy the outdoors?

_____

_____

_____

_____

What is the most incredible thing you've ever seen in nature?

_____

_____

_____

_____

_____

What is something you want to protect in the environment?

_____

_____

_____

What is your favorite way to enjoy the outdoors?

_____

_____

_____

What is the most incredible thing you've ever seen in nature?

_____

_____

_____

_____

# MOM

Who is someone that doesn't live nearby that you wish you could spend more time with? What is special about your relationship because they live far away?

_____

_____

_____

_____

_____

_____

_____

_____

_____

_____

_____

_____

Who is someone that doesn't live nearby that you wish you could spend more time with? What is special about your relationship because they live far away?

_____

_____

_____

_____

_____

_____

_____

_____

_____

_____

_____

# MOM

Write down five things you're grateful for that you can touch.

_____

_____

_____

_____

_____

Write down five things you're grateful for that you can't touch.

_____

_____

_____

_____

_____

Write down five things you're grateful for that you can touch.

_____

_____

_____

_____

_____

Write down five things you're grateful for that you can't touch.

_____

_____

_____

_____

_____

Who is someone in your family you think you could appreciate more? What about them makes you think so?

_____

_____

_____

_____

Whose contributions to the world do you appreciate despite having never met that person?

_____

_____

_____

_____

Who is someone that works hard to make your community a better place?

_____

_____

_____

# DAUGHTER

Who is someone in your family you think you could appreciate more? What about them makes you think so?

_____

_____

_____

_____

Whose contributions to the world do you appreciate despite having never met that person?

_____

_____

_____

_____

Who is someone that works hard to make your school a better place?

_____

_____

_____

What is your favorite season? Write about how it makes you feel and why.

_____

_____

_____

_____

_____

_____

_____

_____

_____

_____

_____

_____

_____

What is your favorite season? Write about how it makes you feel and why.

_____

_____

_____

_____

_____

_____

_____

_____

_____

_____

_____

_____

_____

_____

What is a charity you support or would like to support? Why?

_____

_____

_____

_____

What do you love most about the country you live in?

_____

_____

_____

_____

What is something you may take for granted about living in your country?

_____

_____

_____

_____

# DAUGHTER

What is a charity you would like to support? Why?

_____

_____

_____

_____

What do you love most about the country you live in?

_____

_____

_____

_____

What is something you may take for granted about living in your country?

_____

_____

_____

_____

# MOM

Free writing space

_____

_____

_____

_____

_____

_____

_____

_____

_____

_____

_____

_____

_____

_____

# DAUGHTER

Free writing space

_____

_____

_____

_____

_____

_____

_____

_____

_____

_____

_____

_____

_____

_____

Who is someone that works hard, but you often don't notice or appreciate them?

_____

_____

Where is a place you are thankful you were able to visit?

_____

_____

_____

A place I would like to take my daughter to see is
_____. I think my daughter would like it
because:

_____

_____

_____

_____

_____

_____

Who is someone that works hard, but you often don't notice or appreciate them?

_____

_____

Where is a place you are thankful you were able to visit?

_____

_____

_____

A place I would like to see with my mom is
_____. I think it would be fun for us because:

_____

_____

_____

_____

_____

_____

Write about a historical figure who you wish you could have known. What do you appreciate about them?

_____

_____

_____

_____

_____

_____

_____

_____

_____

_____

_____

Write about a historical figure who you wish you could have known. What do you appreciate about them?

_____

_____

_____

_____

_____

_____

_____

_____

_____

_____

_____

# MOM

What are five everyday things that aren't available throughout the world that you may take for granted?

_____

_____

_____

_____

_____

Choose one thing on the list and write all the things you appreciate about it.

_____

_____

_____

_____

_____

_____

_____

# DAUGHTER

What are five everyday things that aren't available throughout the world that you may take for granted?

_____

_____

_____

_____

_____

Choose one thing on the list and write all the things you appreciate about it.

_____

_____

_____

_____

_____

_____

_____

What is your favorite animal? What do you appreciate about it?

_____

_____

_____

_____

_____

_____

_____

_____

_____

_____

_____

# DAUGHTER

What is your favorite animal? What do you appreciate about it?

_____

_____

_____

_____

_____

_____

_____

_____

_____

_____

_____

_____

# MOM

When have you seen people rally together to accomplish something?

_____

_____

_____

_____

What is a special skill of yours that you could offer someone going through a tough time?

_____

_____

_____

What is a way you could show appreciation to someone who doesn't speak your language?

_____

_____

_____

_____

# DAUGHTER

When have you seen people rally together to accomplish something?

_____

_____

_____

_____

What is a special skill of yours that you could offer someone going through a tough time?

_____

_____

_____

What is a way you could show appreciation to someone who doesn't speak your language?

_____

_____

_____

_____

# MOM

How is your life different today than a year ago? What are some of the positive changes you are thankful for?

_____

_____

_____

_____

_____

_____

_____

_____

_____

_____

_____

_____

_____

# DAUGHTER

How is your life different today than a year ago? What are some of the positive changes you are thankful for?

_____

_____

_____

_____

_____

_____

_____

_____

_____

_____

_____

_____

# MOM

List five people you want to express your gratitude toward.
How could you do that?

_____

_____

_____

_____

_____

Why is expressing gratitude for others' efforts important?

_____

_____

_____

_____

_____

_____

_____

_____

# DAUGHTER

List five people you want to express your gratitude toward. How could you do that?

_____

_____

_____

_____

_____

Why is expressing gratitude for others' efforts important?

_____

_____

_____

_____

_____

_____

_____

_____

# MOM

What inspires you each day? (It could be a person, website, artwork, nature, etc.)

_____

_____

_____

Where is the most beautiful place you've seen a sunrise or sunset?

_____

_____

_____

What is something you think all teenagers—no matter where they live—have in common?

_____

_____

_____

_____

What inspires you each day? (It could be a person, website, artwork, nature, etc.)

_____

_____

_____

Where is the most beautiful place you've seen a sunrise or sunset?

_____

_____

_____

What do you think all mothers—no matter where they live—have in common?

_____

_____

_____

_____

Sometimes it's difficult to be positive when everything seems to be challenging or going wrong. What are some ways you can easily incorporate gratitude into your routine?

_____

_____

_____

_____

_____

_____

_____

_____

_____

_____

_____

_____

Sometimes life gets busy, and you might lose focus on what's important. What are some ways you can easily incorporate gratitude into your routine now?

_____

_____

_____

_____

_____

_____

_____

_____

_____

_____

_____

_____

_____

_____

_____

Free writing space

# DAUGHTER

Free writing space

# ONE LAST LOOK

Practicing gratitude is a lifelong journey that doesn't end with this book. It's a good idea to reflect upon what you learned during this process, and how you can continue making gratitude a part of your routine. The best part? It's something you can do together to keep your relationship strong.

1.  What did you learn about each other that you didn't know before?

_____

_____

2.  Why are you grateful that you did this together?

_____

_____

3.  How has this book changed your outlook?

_____

_____

4.  How can you continue to practice gratitude regularly?

_____

_____

# ABOUT THE AUTHOR

 **Whitney Fleming** is a writer, social media consultant, and creator of the popular blog *Playdates on Fridays*, where she shares the easy, the hard, and the funny about raising teenagers. Her goal is to share stories that help parents feel less alone in this challenging phase of parenting.

She loves good coffee, good wine, and good food, especially when she can share these experiences with friends and family. She is extremely grateful for her three amazing teen daughters who teach her something new each day; her handsome and understanding husband who always encourages her to chase her dreams; and her disobedient dog, Jax, who never listens but loves her the most. She resides in the suburbs of Chicago and is constantly lobbying to eliminate daylight saving time.

CPSIA information can be obtained
at www.ICGtesting.com
Printed in the USA
JSHW032104020921
18366JS00009B/19